Animals in Love

in

Milly Brown

summersdale

ANIMALS IN LOVE

Summersdale Publishers Ltd
46 West Street
Chichester
West Sussex
PO19 1RP
UK

www.summersdale.com

Printed and bound by Tien Wah Press, Singapore

All images © Shutterstock

ISBN: 978-1-84024-714-5

Animals in Love

All **love** is **sweet**,
given or **returned**.

Percy Bysshe Shelley

You come to **love** not by finding the **perfect** person, but by **seeing** an imperfect person perfectly.

Sam Keen

Life is a **flower** of which love is the **honey.**

Victor Hugo

When two **people** love
each other, they don't **look**
at each other; they look in
the **same direction**.

Ginger Rogers

I **love** you
Not **only** for what **you** are
But for what I am
When **I am** with you...

Roy Croft

A kiss is a **lovely trick** designed by nature to **stop speech** when words become superfluous.

Ingrid Bergman

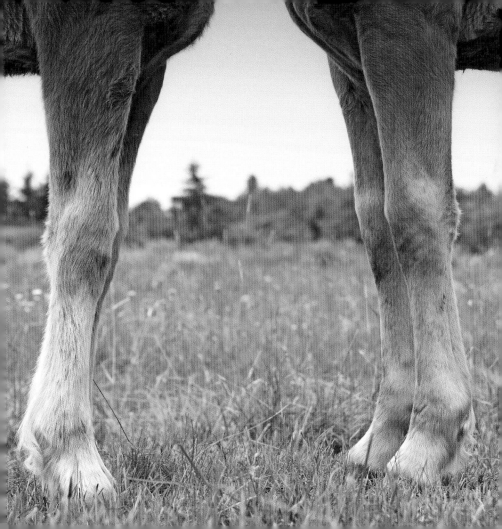

Love vanquishes time. To lovers, **a moment** can be eternity, **eternity** can be the tick of a clock.

Mary Parrish

There will **always** be **romance** in the world so long as there are **young hearts** in it.

Christian Nestell Bovee

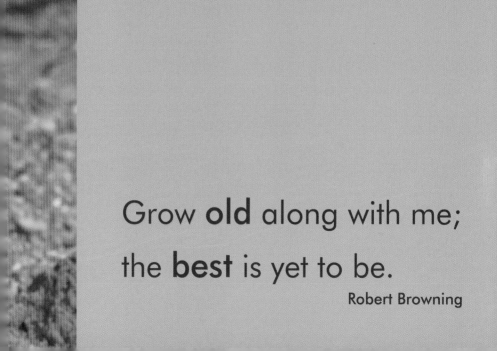

Grow **old** along with me;
the **best** is yet to be.

Robert Browning

Love is a **canvas** furnished by **nature** and embroidered by **imagination.**

Voltaire

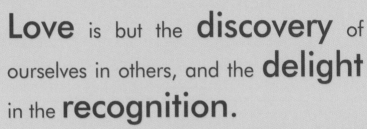

Love is but the **discovery** of ourselves in others, and the **delight** in the **recognition.**

Alexander Smith

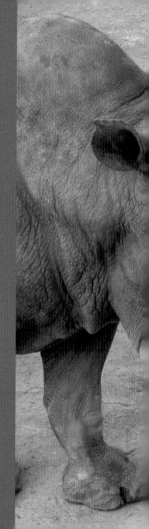

If **grass can grow** through cement, love can find you at **every time** in your life.

Cher

To love and be loved is to **feel the sun** from **both sides.**

David Viscott

We are, each of us, **angels** with only one wing; and we can only fly by **embracing one another.**

Luciano de Crescenzo

Where **there is love** there
is no question.

Albert Einstein

In love the **paradox** occurs that two beings **become one** and yet remain two.

Erich Fromm

Anyone can be **passionate**, but it takes real lovers to be **silly**.

Rose Franken

We **love** because it's the only true **adventure.**

Nikki Giovanni

Love one another and you will be **happy**.
It's as **simple** and as **difficult** as that.

Michael Leunig

My bounty is as **boundless** as the sea,

My love as **deep;** the more I give to thee,

The more I have, for both are **infinite.**

William Shakespeare, *Romeo and Juliet*

Love is **what you make it** and who you make it with.

Mae West

A **kiss** makes
the **heart** young
again and **wipes**
out the years.

Rupert Brooke

One who **walks** the road **with love** will never walk the road alone.

C. T. Davis

Never **close your lips**
to those whom you have
opened your heart.

Charles Dickens

Love is like **pi** – natural, **irrational** and very important.

Lisa Hoffman

The anticipation of **touch** is one of the most potent **sensations** on earth.

Richard J. Finch

Then seek not, **sweet**, the 'If' and 'Why'
I love you now **until I die**.

Christopher Brennan

I love you. **I am at rest** with you. I have come **home.**

Dorothy L. Sayer

I want **love**, because love is the **best feeling** in the whole world.

Fairuza Balk

All **love is original,**
no matter how many other
people have loved before.

George Weinberg

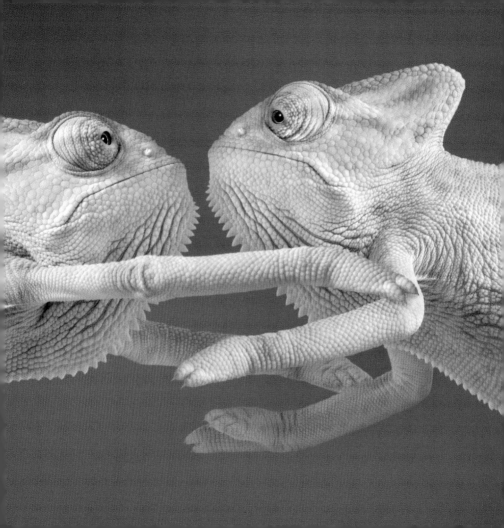

Love at **first sight** is easy to understand; it's when two people have been **looking** at each other **for a lifetime** that it becomes a miracle.

Amy Bloom

If I know what **love** is,

it is because of **you**.

Herman Hesse

You have to walk **carefully** in the **beginning** of love; the running across fields into your **lover's arms** can only come later when you're sure they won't **laugh** if you trip.

Jonathan Carroll

Two souls with but a **single** thought, **two hearts** that beat as one.

Friedrich Halm

Earth's the **right place** for love: I **don't know** where it's likely to go better.

Robert Frost

Lip on **lip,** and eye on eye,
Love to love, **we live,** we die;
No more thou, and no more I,
We, and **only we!**
Richard Monckton Milnes, Lord Houghton

When we are **in love** we seem to ourselves quite **different** from what we were before.

Blaise Pascal

Once you **find love**, you find it. There isn't an **age** on love.

Candace Cameron

Love is like **smiling**; it **never fades** and is contagious.

Paula Dean

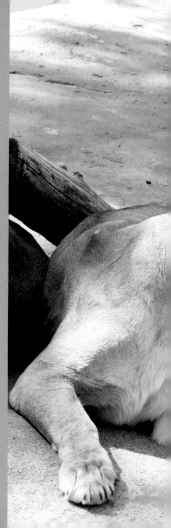

When **I saw you** I fell in love. And **you smiled** because you knew.

Arrigo Boito

To **love deeply**
in one direction
makes us **more**
loving in all others.
Madame Swetchine

I can **summon** at will all my **happiest** hours,

And relive my past **buried** in your lap...

Charles Baudelaire

There is only
one happiness
in life, to **love**
and be **loved.**
George Sand

PHOTO CREDITS

Love Kittens

Milly Brown

Love Kittens

£5.99

ISBN: 978-1-84024-688-9

Is there anything cuter than a cuddly kitten, all fluffy and dewy eyed and looking for love?

Yes. Lots of them!

These picture perfect bundles of fur are guaranteed to melt your heart and put a smile on your face.

Love Puppies

£5.99

ISBN: 978-1-84024-689-6

Is there anything cuter than a cuddly puppy, all fluffy and dewy eyed and looking for love?

Yes. Lots of them! These picture perfect bundles of fur are guaranteed to melt your heart and put a smile on your face.

Combining gorgeous photographs with thoughtful prose, these adorable books really do make the loveliest gifts.

www.summersdale.com